The GREATEST Adventure!

Bunty Bunce

ISBN 978-0-473-35754-2

© Cover and Illustrations by Diana Chetwin, chetwin4@farmside.co.nz
Editing, design & prepress, Briar Whitehead, www.wordsndesign.co.nz
Printed by yourbooks.co.nz, New Zealand

Dedication

Sam represents all the children in the world and I dedicate this book to them. Children everywhere can get to know their Heavenly Father's voice, and place their lives in His loving hands! He wants to protect, encourage and help them at all times. Open your heart to Him, so you can say, just like Sam, "Life is a Great Supernatural Adventure!"

To fall in love with God is the greatest romance, to seek Him the greatest adventure, to find Him the greatest human achievement.

St Augustine

Acknowledgements

I want to thank my Heavenly Father for encouraging me to write down what He has done for me. His patience and love kept me going. "Thank you Father!" I now want to thank Hope Martin for the hours she spent helping me work through these many stories. Thanks Hope. Also Diana Chetwin, Elaine Cleland, Annette Yeatman, Judy Bird, Miriam Fawcet, Di Brown, Geoff and Winifred Fawcet, Rob and Deb Buxton, Louise Tregidga, Helen Thiam, Richard Harris and all those people who have prayed for me over these past few weeks. God bless you for cheering me on!

Endorsements

I grew up listening to Bunty's stories of what God was doing through her life. They excited me. I wanted to see God working wonders through my life as He was through Bunty's. When I was 16, Bunty invited me to accompany her on a six months trip around the world. That trip was the beginning of my service in missions and one of the happiest, funniest and most fruitful times of ministry. I learned from Bunty how to pray and see immediate answers, how to serve in different cultures and how to make room for the Holy Spirit at every opportunity. I hope this book touches and encourages you as much as Bunty's life has touched and encouraged me.

Nathanael Edwards
Minister at The Community Church, Storrington, UK
Director of Life Support, a charity working in Zambia, Africa

This delightful book of Bunty's reveals the heart of the Father in His interaction with His children. As Bunty weaves her own testimony into these stories, we gain a greater understanding of God's amazing love for children everywhere and His desire to have an intimate relationship with each one. It will stir your heart, challenge your faith and spark a desire to know His voice as Bunty does."

Felicity Tucker, Children's Ministry,
Freedom Church, Porirua, NZ

The Greatest Adventure is truly an amazing story that brings a message to everyone. Sam represents each of us, whether man or woman, boy or girl. She teaches us how to hear from God and also how to respond to him. Just as Sam (really Bunty Bunce) journeyed with God, we discover He also wants to journey with each of us. As you read this book, open your heart and spirit to hear His voice and discover His plan for your life – it will change you forever, just as it did for Sam.

Naomi Dowdy, Former Senior Pastor, Trinity Christian Centre,
Singapore

The Greatest Adventure

Some of Bunty's adventures are described in her first book, *In My Father's Hands*. In *The Greatest Adventure*, Sam, the girl in the book, has more of Bunty's adventures. Bunty wants every boy and girl to identify with Sam in her experiences of the love and friendship of Jesus and follow her into a supernatural relationship with God! He is alive today! What He has done for Sam He can do for them.

Foreword

IT is a great joy and honor for me to write the foreword to this book, *The Greatest Adventure!* Bunty Bunce (the true identity of Sam in this book) has been a dear friend, fellow spiritual adventurer, and an inspiring role model to my husband (Jan) and to me.

We first met in Colorado Springs, USA, at a house meeting for women in ministry. My role there (as a seminary professor) was to encourage these precious handmaidens of the Lord by showing them from the original Hebrew and Greek Scriptures about God's great love for girls and women and teaching the Biblical theology of God's call and equipping of women to minister and lead in Christ's kingdom. I enjoyed meeting these wonderful women and sharing from the Word of God, but I never anticipated receiving such a precious gift at that event. A gift that would be life changing—friendship with Bunty Bunce!

Meeting Bunty that day and growing to know her better and better through the years since then is like getting to know a New Testament character who stepped right out of the Book of Acts—like Priscilla ... or Dorcas ... or the four prophesying daughters of Philip. Here is a 21st century woman living a first-century apostolic Christ life—full of the Spirit and full of adventure!

From first hearing the stories Bunty shared, from having her in our home, to travelling with her in ministry, the joy of Jesus, the glow of the Spirit and the experience of adventure have only increased. Kids love adventure—and Bunty loves kids! I can testify that Bunty Bunce, this "God's gal", is the real thing!

I can also testify that I have been learning from Bunty! She knows Jesus, His voice, and helps others to learn how to hear it. In this book she shares her story—as simply as a child can understand (and that includes me!)—how you can learn to hear His voice, too ... how you can discern God's will for your life ... how you can see what God wants and participate in bringing it about ... how you can learn to trust God and find your needs fulfilled ... and best of all, how you can learn to know and love the Father and become best friends!

Now I invite you to embark on a spiritual adventure of your own with the guidance of the bubbly, bouncy, bundle of life, Bunty Bunce. Spiritual adventures aren't just for adults. Many of the greatest life-long adventures began with an invitation to a child from the Heavenly Father. Perhaps, in this book, you will hear the invitation. It all begins by being found by God.

Deborah M. Gill
Professor, Biblical Studies and Exposition
Assemblies of God Theological Seminary

Contents

The Father's Love 13

The Father's Friendship 15

The Father's Sacrifice 20

The Father's Voice 23

The Father's Patience 25

The Father's Will 28

The Father's Call 31

The Father's Provision... 34

The Father's Compassion 36

The Father's Cry 39

The Father's Faith.. 41

The Father's Vision.. 46

The Father's Faithfulness...................................... 50

The Father's Adventure 55

The Father's Joy 58

The Father's Message 62

The Father's Promise... 66

The Father's Hand... 69

The Father's Surprise 71

The Father's Word 75

The Father's Heart 83

The Father's Persistence 86

The Father's Encouragement 89

The Father's Language 91

The Father's Invitation 95

The Father's Assignment 100

The Father's Photo 103

The Father's Choice 107

The Father's House 110

The Author's Comments 114

The Father's Desire 116

Bible Verses to Learn 117

The Father's Love

*"Of all the animals a lamb best represents
my love for the world," the Father said.*

"A lamb?" said Sam. "I don't understand."

LOOKING up into her Father's eyes one day Sam asked Him,
"Father, why are there stars?"

"They are there to remind you that I am always looking down
on you," He said.

"Why are there clouds?" asked Sam.

" They are there to remind you that I am always moving above
you."

"What about the birds?"

"They remind you how free you can be in my presence as I move above you and look down on you."

"The trees?" she said excitedly.

"That's to show you I have given you creation to enjoy."

"Father, what about the animals?"

"The animals – I love the animals. One of them represents my love for the world.

"I created everything and I enjoy everything I have created. From the beginning of time till now I have been watching, and hovering over the earth, looking down from heaven upon my creation and wondering, 'Is all well?' From the dawning of the day, until the sun goes down, I look after everything I have made. I was there at the beginning and I will be there at the end. I AM the Beginning and the End, the Alpha and the Omega, the First and the Last. I am Eternal. I was never born and I will never die. I have always been, and am and will be. There is no ending to my love for the world. In fact, there isn't any other God."

"Father, thank you so much for creating everything – but you mentioned something about an animal. What animal represents your love for the world?" asked Sam.

"Oh, the lamb, Sam. The lamb represents my love for the world."

"The lamb? I don't understand."

"All in good time Sam. I will explain everything in good time."

The Father's Friendship

God, if you live in heaven
please show me a sign?"

SAM hadn't always talked to her Heavenly Father like this. She grew up in the south of England, near London, not knowing her father, and barely knowing her mother. During her first seven years, she lived in two orphanages (homes where children live together who come from broken families). After that she went to stay with her grandmother and mother in London. She was a very quiet child, always watching and listening.

When she was twelve years old, she was taken to a children's holiday camp where people were talking about God. Who was He? Where was He? Why was He? Sitting with other children during one of these meetings, she noticed the teacher picking up a big book. It was the Bible. Slowly the teacher turned to the book of Genesis and began to read the story of Adam and Eve.

She explained how God had created them and placed them in a beautiful garden and told them not to eat the fruit of a particular tree. But Satan, in the form of a snake whispered to them to eat it. They ate it and then they hid behind a bush. The Bible says God began to walk around the garden looking for them. He called, "Adam, where are you?" "We're hiding," they answered. "We listened to Satan and we sinned, so we are hiding from you."

"After Adam and Eve listened to Satan and disobeyed God, God sent them out of the garden. Because of what he had done Satan became God's biggest enemy and God had a choice to make. d could sit down and feel sorry for Himself, or do something about it. Like a lion awaking from sleep, He stretched His arms, took a deep breath and roared into the Universe, 'I have a plan!'"

The teacher continued.

"God knew the only way of stopping Satan deceiving the whole world was to become human like Adam and Eve and face the temptations they faced, but without sinning, and that is exactly what He did.

"In God's perfect timing, He planted a supernatural seed in the womb of a young girl called Mary. It wasn't long before she realised she was pregnant. She wasn't married at the time, but an angel came and told Joseph, her future husband, not to reject her. He told him that the Holy Spirit of God had put His seed inside her and the baby boy who would be born was to be called Jesus, and would rescue everyone from their sins. So Joseph married her.

"Jesus grew up and was known as the Son of God, because God's Holy Spirit had created Him. He was sinless. He was also named Emmanuel, which means, 'God with us.' From that moment God came to this earth, as a man, and lived with us."

As Sam listened intently, God's presence began to surround her. She felt lovely and warm. She knew He was real and the desire to be His friend gripped her.

The teacher continued. "Jesus grew up and often spoke to people about heaven and the heart of God. Many rejected Him but others accepted Him. He would tell the people He was the Way, the Truth and the Life and the only way to know the Father, but the people would laugh at Him. A time came when the crowds began to hate Him. In fact, they even wanted to kill Him! He had healed the sick, opened blind eyes, and made lame people walk! He had even raised the dead to show them that He was from heaven, but they turned their backs on Him.

Finally He was arrested and nailed onto a wooden cross to die. The people mocked Him because He had been named the King of the Jews.

Jesus, full of pain, looked over the crowds and then to heaven and prayed, 'Father, forgive them, they don't know what they are doing'. Not long after that He died.

"But then," said the teacher her voice rising with excitement, "three days later Jesus rose from the dead! God's Spirit inside Him was so strong, that He smashed death and came back to life and walked out of the tomb!"

Sam could hardly stay sitting down. As she listened wide-eyed, the teacher continued. "Death was now conquered. Sin had been destroyed and the grave was now empty. Jesus was alive! God's power had overcome Satan's."

At this point the teacher got so excited that she nearly jumped over the bench Sam was sitting on!

The atmosphere in the room was very quiet. The children were really listening. Looking around the group the teacher asked if any of them had made friends with Jesus and if so, would they be willing to stand up and say what He had done for them. One child stood up and said, "I thank the Lord Jesus, for dying for me."

"I thank Him for forgiving me for everything I have done wrong," said a voice behind Sam. Another said, "I thank Him for rising from the dead."

A fourth child said, "I thank Him for being here with us right now."

When Sam heard this, she felt someone come and sit down beside her. She turned to look. She saw no one, but she knew it was Jesus. As she closed her eyes, her heart began to pound and her mind raced.

"Sam! Sam! What are you going to do? He's here! He's here!" she said to herself. Jumping to her feet, she shouted, "Lord Jesus, forgive my sins and come into my life." As she said this, warmth and love filled her. It felt like the person who was sitting beside her had risen to His feet, given her a hug and completely filled her up inside. She was speechless.

Tears came to her eyes. She knew the God of heaven had found her. She was not hiding behind a bush like Adam and Eve. Her sins were forgiven. She felt a wonderful peace.

She went outside and looking up into the dark sky prayed, "God, in school we pray a prayer called, the 'Lord's Prayer'. If you live in heaven and you have something to do with Jesus, who I have just been learning about, please show me a sign?" Slowly, stars began to form in a circle above the camp. She smiled. She knew no one else could do that. She began to think about Jesus and what He had done for her. Knowing He was alive and filling her heart, she spoke to Him, "Lord Jesus, you gave your life for me. I want to give my life for you." A deep peace saturated her. She and God weren't strangers any more. She was His friend. She wasn't longing any more for someone she couldn't find. He was with her, right beside her and within her.

Words and feelings tumbled around inside her.

"Time? What is Time? Time is now.

"Where is He? Where has He gone? He is living inside me. He is settling down into His new home.

"Love. What is love? He is love."

As God's love filled Sam's heart she spoke to her Heavenly Father, "I want to be your friend. I want to be with you forever. I want to obey you. I want to love you and make your heart happy. I don't want to be like Adam and Eve, but Lord, I want to follow you."

Hearing Sam's prayer, the Father smiled. She was His child, and as her Heavenly Father, He would care for her all the days of her life, never leaving or forsaking her. He would be with her forever!

The Father's Sacrifice

Sam learns about the Lamb

SAM began to go to church and meet with other believers. She would hear people teaching from the Bible and slowly she grew to love Jesus with all her heart.

One sermon really excited her.

The preacher began, "After Adam and Eve had left the garden, they had children, and the children had children, and it wasn't long before a nation was born. God journeyed with this nation.

"He asked the priests to sacrifice a lamb and offer the blood of the lamb to God to cover their sins for a year. They did this, but the people still drifted away from loving the true and living God and began to worship idols they had made.

"As each generation of people lived and died without knowing Him, God knew the only answer was to send His Son Jesus down to earth to show us the way back to Him. That's why Jesus was called the Lamb of God. He was sacrificed instead of us, nailed to a wooden cross. As this huge burden was put onto Him, Jesus cried out to God, 'My God! My God! Why have you forsaken me?' The world's sin had separated Jesus from God. He suffered and died, but three days later He rose from the dead. No more separation. The power of sin had been broken!"

Just then Sam remembered her conversation with the Lord.

"Father! Father! Now I know what you meant! The animal that represented your love for the world was the Lamb! Jesus was your Lamb! He gave His life for the sins of the world!" said Sam excitedly.

"Yes. That's exactly what He did. He was the Lamb that destroyed the effects of Adam's sin. He was pure and had never done anything wrong – a perfect sacrifice. He laid His life down; no one took it from Him. Because of His love for you He wanted to do this, die on a cross instead of you. It filled Him with joy to do that for you. He could have called 10,000 angels to rescue Him but He didn't even ask for one! He knew if He took the punishment for the world's sin, just once for everybody for all time, those who trusted Him could be forgiven and their sins could be washed away in His blood. Now Adam's sin has been dealt with. Satan's control over you has been broken, and people can have eternal life with me again. They can know me and love me, and together we can have a relationship, just like I am having with you."

Sam felt completely overwhelmed.

"Oh Father, thank you so much for loving me! Thank you for sending Jesus! Thank you that His blood has washed away everything I have ever done wrong. Thank you for being my friend! I want to know you as you know me! I want to taste and see that you are good, all the time!"

The Father's Voice

Father, I want to follow you ...

FOR Sam to go where God told her, she needed to be able to hear His voice.

She prayed. "Father, please teach me to hear your voice so I can follow you.

As Sam made her way to school, she sked Him, "How long will I have to wait at the bus stop before the bus comes?"

The first thought she had was, "ten minutes", but the bus came in twenty!

"Lord, that can't have been your voice, because you always tell the truth. I am now late for school. Will there be someone on the gate to book me?"

"Yes," was her first thought. Thirty minutes later she arrived at the gate, but no one was there.

"Lord, that wasn't your voice either. Please teach me to hear your voice," she pleaded.

For a whole week she prayed like this and every time she thought it was His voice, it wasn't.

The following week, she prayed the same prayers. "When will the next bus come?"

"Ten minutes," came the reply, and in ten minutes the bus arrived.

"Will there be someone at the school gates?" she would ask.

"No," came the reply, and it was true. There wasn't anyone at the school gates. For the whole week everything turned out just as she thought.

To confirm His voice to her, she did the same the third week. She prayed, got an answer, and what she heard was what happened. Now she knew, without a shadow of a doubt, she could hear His voice.

When evening came she knelt down by her bed. "Lord," she said. "I won't pray silly prayers anymore, because I know I can hear your voice. Thank you so much for teaching me. Speak Lord, for I love to hear your voice."

From that day forward Sam found it easy to hear God speak to her, and easy to speak to Him. The Bible says He is the Good Shepherd and we are His sheep. His sheep hear His voice and follow after Him.

The Father's Patience

I've got better things for you
than gold medals ...

"HEY Sam! Hello there! Where are you? Can you hear me?"

Time had passed, and Sam was enjoying all sorts of things. She wasn't quite as tuned in as she had been to God's voice. "Hey Sam? Hello there? Do you hear me?" No response.

Saddened, He kept calling her name. "Sam? Sam? Where are you? I am waiting patiently for you."

Realising it was the voice of her Father, Sam stopped what she was doing. Slowly tilting her head upwards, and looking at Him, she said, "Yes Lord?"

"Sam, I have been wanting to speak with you. There is so much on my heart. I would like to share it with you, because you are my friend. You aren't my servant, you're my friend!"

Sam, realising she was God's friend, had forgotten His heartache for the world. She had been enjoying life, and without knowing it she had been drifting slowly away from His love.

"Father, I am so sorry. I have become preoccupied with so many other things. There is so much to see in the shops, and places to go, and friends to meet up with. I joined an athletic club and began to throw the javelin. You should have seen me. I was even picked to represent Britain and I threw against Germany and Sweden. You would have been proud of me!"

Her Father, after lovingly and patiently listening to Sam's happy chatter, began to share His heart.

"Sam, I was there when you were in the shops and meeting with your friends. I was there when you joined the athletic club, and spent many evenings training. Even as the sun was setting, I saw you running through the streets of London to your home, and then snuggling down to sleep. I was even there in Sweden when you threw the javelin for Britain. I watched quietly, and waited patiently for you to remember me.

"Sam, the things you see, and your successes and achievements can take you away from me. These things can fill up your heart but they are temporary, not eternal. You cannot take the things you buy in the shops, or the gold medals you win on the sports field to heaven with you. You cannot take your friends with you either, if they haven't already met me.

"Sam, spend your time seeking me. Set your mind on things above, not on things of the earth. For the things of the world will disappear, but my things will last forever. Store up treasures in heaven. There are no moths or rust there, and burglars can't break in and steal them. Your heart will be wherever your treasure is. I will show you the path of life. In my presence you will be full of joy and have wonderful pleasures to enjoy. Get to know me with all of your heart, soul, mind and strength. Love other people as you love me and let me fill you with my joy."

Sam, encouraged by her Father's love, wanted more than anything to continue to serve and love Him. To go to all her neighbours, far and wide, with His love and joy was now her deepest desire.

"Father, thank you for understanding me. You surround me on all sides and you've placed your hand upon me. I can't get away from you and I don't want to. If I go up to heaven you are there. If I go to the bottom of the sea you are there. Wherever I am, you are. It's all too wonderful for me. Thank you Father for your patience, love and joy. Thank you for drawing me closer to you. Thank you for being my friend!"

The Father's Will

... a van was not really Sam's idea
of comfortable accommodation

FOR Sam to do what God wanted, she needed to understand how
He was leading her.

The Bible tells us that the best thing we can do is to give all of
ourselves to God and to think His way and not the way that other
people think. He will change us from the inside out and show us
His good plans for us.

As Sam began to talk to God she started to understand what
His plans for her were.

While she was studying at Bible College she wanted to do
God's will, in the little things as well as the big things. But what
God wanted and what she wanted weren't always the same thing.

Once, during her school break she was given a choice. She was invited to travel with a ministry team around England, sleeping in a van, or she could accept a position at a church where she would be living with a family and sleeping in a house.

God had been talking to Sam about church. "A church is another name for people who gather together to learn about me," He had told her. "I am the head of the church and the people are like my body. I lead them and guide them. We journey through life and eternity together."

"Father," she prayed. "Would you like me to travel around England, or can I go to Bracknell, and help in my friend's church."

As time went by Sam knew she should accept the invitation to travel with the ministry team and travel around the country sleeping in a van, but she didn't like the thought of sleeping in a van. "Surely, He wouldn't want me to do that," she thought. She decided to accept the church position, and live with a family in a house.

So, that decision made, she jumped on her motorbike and travelled to Bracknell, just outside London.

While she was there a funny thing happened! She kept getting confused at the roundabouts on the way to the church. Three roundabouts flowed into each other. After two weeks of losing her way on the roundabouts she began to get the message. She had made the wrong decision: she had chosen comfort over inconvenience. She knew God's will was not confusing, but here she was getting confused every day!

"Father," she prayed. "I know you wanted me to travel the country and tell others about your love, and sleep in a van, but I wanted comfort Lord. I grew up in a children's home and when I came out, my mother didn't have a very nice house. The wallpaper was dark brown and the carpets were the same. Father, it was such a nice thought to be safe and sound in a house, with a family, ministering in a church. Forgive me Father. Your thoughts are not my thoughts and your ways are not my ways.

"Lord, please give to me today what you were going to give to me later, and give to me later what you were going to give me today. I ask you Lord, to reverse your plans for me, and bring me into your will. Thank you Father."

The following day Sam jumped on her motorbike, and to her great surprise navigated the roundabouts. Now in God's perfect will, joy began to flow through her. His 'will' brought joy to her heart.

She helped and loved the elderly in the church for three months, and a year later travelled the country ministering in villages and cities, sleeping in many different types of beds and accommodation. The Lord had reversed His training program in her life. He knows how to bring good out of every situation.

A few years later as Sam was standing on a pavement square, looking into a shop window, the presence of the Lord came all about her and suddenly she knew she was in the very centre of her Father's will. Tears ran down her cheeks as she realised that moving to the pavement square to the left, or right of her would have taken her out of His will. That exact pavement square, exact shop window, at that exact time, was where God wanted her to be. Out of the whole world that was where He wanted her! Because she wanted so much to be aware of His will, God trained her to be sensitive in every situation in which she found herself – the little, as well as the big. Sam continued to ask herself, "Is this His will? Or is this?" forever conscious of doing whatever it was that most pleased Him, even if it meant standing on one pavement square! She discovered that when she was doing what He wanted she felt alive and full of energy.

The Father's Call

*"Sam," the Father asked, "would you be
willing to go all over the world and talk
about the good news of my love?"*

"I will never leave you or forsake you," the Father said to her
lovingly one day. "You will always have enough money to do the
things I ask. I will be your health and comfort. I will encourage
you when you feel down and I will send my angels to watch
over you all the time. If you are lonely I will bring along people
to accompany you. I will be your faith and when you pray to me

I will answer you. If you are ever fearful I will give you strength and courage, and I will be your protector. I will be with you day and night, and watch over you as you sleep. You may have to climb high mountains. You may have to walk through deep valleys, but I will always be with you. I will never leave you or forsake you. You may travel to faraway places and your life may be in danger, but you don't need to worry, because I am the resurrection and the life. He who loses his life for my sake will find it again, for I have overcome death and destruction. I am eternal and give eternal life to those who believe in me. Would you be willing to leave your family and loved ones and work for me? I will give you the faith of Daniel and Samuel and send you to many nations and ask you to speak for me. You may be afraid of the people's faces and you may not know their languages, but I will give you interpreters who will travel with you and introduce you to the right people. So don't fear their cultures, or where you will sleep at night, or the food put before you, for I will be with you. I will instruct you and teach you in the way you should go and I will guide you. Will you go for me?"

As Sam sat quietly in the presence of God, she thought about His invitation to her. "If He gave His life for me, I should give my life for Him," she reflected.

Weighing up all the consequences of leaving family and friends, sleeping in unusual places, eating strange food, and living out of a suitcase, she decided to trust Him.

"Father," she said, "this day I would like to surrender my todays and tomorrows to you. Yes, lead me and guide me. I give you full permission to be my everything. Be my friend. Be my Lord. Be my Saviour, counsellor, teacher, father, God, my all. I will go where you want me to go. I will do what you want me to do. I will say what you want me to say. Your will, not mine be done. Please give me your strength and courage, and I will love and serve you."

With a big smile in His heart, Jesus welcomed her to His journey of Life, in which His peace, love, joy, patience, faith, kindness, and angels, would accompany her. With a joyful heart God began to reveal His plans to her. They were plans of peace and not turmoil, plans for a future full of hope.

The Father's Provision

*So don't worry about your life, what to
eat, or drink, or wear! You are much
more precious than lilies and look how
beautiful they are ...*

AS Sam travelled from nation to nation, she needed money.

While she was at Bible School God trained Sam to trust Him
for all her physical needs. One day she needed £20. She prayed.
The next day a businessman gave her £20. God had spoken to one
of His children, he obeyed, and Sam received an answer to her
prayer.

A little later she needed another £20. She prayed and a woman contacted her saying she had meant to give it to her weeks before but had forgotten, and handed her an envelope containing £20. Again God had heard Sam's prayer for money. Time after time she would ask God to cover all her expenses and He did.

Then Sam was given the opportunity to work as a photographer for a modelling agency in Atlanta, Georgia. Before responding, she checked it out with God. "Father, should I let the agency know that I am available to work for them?" After a few seconds, eyes closed, a picture of a red jacket, with a hand going in and out of a pocket, filled her mind.

"My pocket is your pocket; has been, and always will be!" came His reassuring reply. Sam knew immediately what He meant. "I am going to provide for you my way but not your way!" Sam never applied for the job.

From that day to this, whenever Sam is asked to go on a journey, she makes her need for money known to God. In His faithfulness, He always provides.

If you want to be with Him doing what He wants, He will care for you. You can't please Him without faith and it takes faith to believe that He exists and that He rewards those who really want to get to know Him.

How much does He care for the lilies of the field? They don't work hard but they still grow, and look how beautiful they are. Are you not more precious to Him than them? So do not worry about your life, what you eat, what you drink, what you wear. Your Heavenly Father knows that you need these things.

So first of all, get to know Him and what He wants, and everything you need will be given to you. He takes delight in you because you are His child. Acknowledge Him in all you do and He will guide you and answer your prayers.

The Father's Compassion

Please wipe my tears away and heal my heart.
Show me the way forward ...

SAM, didn't just have to trust God for money; she also had to trust Him to help her with her fears.

The cost of leaving family and friends, going to different countries, and facing new cultures and lifestyles, brought its own set of personal struggles.

"Sam?"

"Yes, Lord?"

"I see your heart is sad today. George has been a good friend to you, and you wondered whether you might marry him, but you realised he was not the one for you. I see how sad you are, but I am about to show you more of what I want you to do."

"Lord, what do you want me to do? Up to this moment I was thinking of marrying George, but Lord, that's not going to happen. Please wipe my tears away and heal my heart. Show me the way forward. Thank you Father."

Now that her relationship with George was over Sam was open to a new direction for her life. She attended a conference and during a seminar, she heard the speaker say, "The bridges around your life have collapsed. Rededicate your life to God."

"Sam! This man is speaking to you, listen to him," she said to herself. Sitting upright, she opened herself up wide to what God was saying. At the end the speaker invited people to stand. As she made herself available to God again for whatever He wanted, she immediately saw a picture in her mind. There were trees growing on a hill, outlined by a beautiful orange sunset. "Lord, I have never seen a hill like this. If this hill is in England, I will go, or if it is in America, I will go. Wherever this hill is, I will go for you!" she exclaimed.

"Sam," said the Lord gently. "I gave you that picture to let you know I have heard your prayer and am about to lead you on a good path. Don't look to the left or right, but straight ahead. For I have planned your days, and they are all written in my book! Those who trust in me will be like a tree planted by a river. They will not fear the heat or the drought. They will continually produce fruit. Trust in me with all your heart and don't try to understand everything, even if the situations you find yourself in are challenging, for I will be with you."

So God taught Sam how to trust Him in all sorts of ways. On one occasion, at Bible School, Sam counselled a lady who was very depressed. As they talked it became clear that her deep involvement in witchcraft had affected her mind. She wanted to give her life to Jesus, but couldn't bring herself to make that commitment. There was a fight for her soul – and she was even thinking of suicide.

At the same time, Sam's mother was constantly phoning and harassing her. Attacked on every side, Sam could only turn to Jesus. "God. I don't understand what's going on," she cried out, "but I know you love me, so I will trust you."

For three weeks this was all she could pray, and the Bible – God's Word – became her lifeline. Eventually, the woman stopped contacting her and Sam's mum stopped phoning.

Sam spent hours in the chapel with God and He comforted and strengthened her.

"Sam," the Father said, "from now on I want you to trust me all the time. Tell me absolutely everything. I will be your refuge and shelter."

Surrounded by a sense of security and love, she knew she could draw near to Him. His strength was stronger than her tears, and His plans were better than hers. Quietly and confidently Sam placed her full trust in Jesus, the one who loved her and gave His life for her, the one who rose from the dead and was alive forever and praying for her.

The Father's Cry

... the children are like sheep without a shepherd

"FATHER, is your heart moved when a child cries?"

"Yes, Sam. When a child cries my heart cries with them. I cry with those who cry and I am joyful when they are joyful."

"But Father, they are just children. Why do you love them so much?"

"While I was walking on the earth, I asked my friends to bring little children to me. The children are like sheep without a shepherd."

"Sheep?" inquired Sam.

"Yes. Sheep! If they are not cared for they will fall into danger. They may go to drink from a river and get caught in the current and swept away, or walk on a mountain pathway, lose their footing and roll down the hill. Yes, sheep need a leader they can follow who will also keep them safe. That's why I came down to the earth.

"I became the Good Shepherd and I gave my life for my sheep. If they follow me they will never lose their footing. I will lead them on safe paths and they will know me and recognise my voice and follow me. I will watch over them night and day and feed them when they are hungry and heal them when they are sick. I will care for them as a father cares for His children."

"Jesus, thank you for loving the little children. Help me to love them with the love you have," said Sam.

The Father's Faith

He took away the bugs and gave Sam a cow!

"SAM, please would you go to Africa and visit Zimbabwe for me? There is an orphanage that needs help. The children have come from very sad backgrounds but I love them. Will you go and show them my love?"

"Lord, I have heard your heart cry for the world, so I will definitely go to Zimbabwe. I want everyone, everywhere to get to know you, so they can put their trust in you and know you as I do. I want them to experience your love, peace and joy and to receive your free gift of eternal life. I don't want anyone to miss out on all the lovely things you have prepared for them. I want them to be with you forever."

With her heart set on Zimbabwe, she made her way to London airport. With tears in her eyes she told her friend that she didn't really know where she was going, only that God wanted her there! But courage began to grow in her heart. At the airport she wiped her eyes and boarded the plane for Zimbabwe, Africa.

On arrival, Sam and senior orphanage staff drove twenty miles out of the city of Harare into the rural areas. Forty-five minutes into the trip Sam got a shock! She saw mud huts, hot and humid skies, and dark-skinned people all around her. But beside this, guess what she saw? Yes! Straight ahead were trees growing on a hill, outlined by a beautiful orange sunset – the picture God had shown her at the conference in England, six months earlier!

"Father," Sam said. "How did you place that scenery in my mind six months ago and bring it into reality today?"

"With me the impossible is possible! I showed you that picture because I knew you were going to see it. I live in the future, as well as the past and present. If you hold my words in your heart and believe that I am able to bring them to pass, they will. That is called faith. If you have faith the size of a tiny mustard seed and tell a mountain to shift, it will. You hope for something and faith brings it to pass, even though it hasn't happened yet, faith already sees it.

"A mustard seed is very small, so your faith doesn't have to be very big. Commit your future to me, and trust me, I will bring to pass all that I have revealed and promised to you. Have faith in me."

"Wow, Lord."

It wasn't long before Sam was asked to speak to a lunchtime Bible Class at a school 20 minutes away.

As she stood apprehensively by the car with a suitcase of library books in one hand, and a suitcase of children's materials in the other, Sam looked up to heaven and prayed, "Lord, let's go!"

"Sam! What do you mean, 'Let's go!' I am not coming with you, you are coming with me!" the Father said.

"Me, coming with you?"

"Yes, I am not going with you. You are coming with me!"

Sam realised she still had a lot to learn. She never thought God had to lead *her*, she thought she just had to pray and ask Him to come *with* her.

When Sam arrived at the school 18 children were waiting for her in a classroom. She told them a Bible story and asked if any of them would like to make friends with Jesus.

At that moment all the children began to cry and some fell on their knees and prayed loudly for God to forgive them and take their sins away.

Sam was stunned. "Lord, how did you know that was going to happen? I went to Bible School but they didn't teach me that you could speak to little children and make them cry out to you like that."

"Sam, I am always looking down from heaven and watching everyone on earth. I know their names and everything about them. When I saw this group of young people, I knew I could trust you to go and share my love with them.

"When you asked me to go with you, I knew I had to show you that this was my idea first. You didn't plan this outreach, I did! I prepared it before I created the earth!"

"Father, you really went ahead of me. You prepared the students' hearts to receive your word. You drew them to yourself.

43

You gathered them in that classroom. You just wanted me to be there and see how good you are.

"Please continue to teach me and guide me. Be my leader. Lead me and I will follow."

As Sam settled into her new nation and orphanage, she was invited to a Bible study. The study was held at a nearby farm. She sat on a couch with three other people, and right above her head, a bright light glared. As it grew darker outside, the light seemed to get brighter, and soon the whole room was filled with bugs!

England wasn't filled with big insects like these, so this was quite a shock for Sam. They ran across the floor; hit the walls; flew into the light above her and crashed-landed in her Bible! Long brown things, called "bombers" by the local people, were smashing into everything and they all seemed to be landing on Sam! "What a welcome to the country," she thought. "All creation wants to greet me!"

That evening Sam returned to her room and climbed into bed. As she turned off her light, her imagination conjured up a foot-long black cockroach on the wall by her bed. Alarmed, she turned the light on and stared at the place on the wall. But it wasn't there. "Oh no! I must have bugs in my room!" she thought nervously.

The more she thought about it the worse it got, until she was too terrified to go to sleep and stayed awake all night on "bug watch"! The following day she decided to move her bed to face the opposite wall.

The next night she inspected the wall anxiously before she turned off the light. "Here goes!" As the light clicked off she was convinced she saw an even bigger creepy-crawly with two monstrous antennae! Sam yanked the string again to turn the light back on and stared at the wall. But it wasn't there. Again, she lay awake all night, wondering if it was running loose in her room!

The following day was Sunday, and the staff from the orphanage were asked to travel to a church meeting. During the service Sam was so tired she began to cry. After confiding in the orphanage staff about her nightly adventures with enormous imaginary bugs they invited her to choose another bedroom.

That evening, in the new bedroom, Sam crawled into bed and her friend asked God to protect Sam from the bugs and give her His peace.

As her friend left the room, Sam looked uneasily at the wall ahead of her and switched off the light – this time in slow motion. Immediately, on the wall facing her, she saw a brown and white English cow munching grass. It was so vivid Sam could hear it. She smiled. It reminded her of home. It was so comforting and peaceful she closed her eyes and went straight to sleep! God was so good – He took away the bugs and gave her a cow.

The test came later, when she was asked to speak one evening to labourers on a coffee plantation in Kenya. As she stood in the crowd waiting her cue, she saw a large gaslight hanging above the platform attracting hundreds of beetles.

"Soon, I'll be out there and those beetles are going to be all over me," Sam thought uneasily.

"Lord" she prayed. "Please prove to me that I have no more fear of bugs. I know what you did for me in Zimbabwe, please reassure me now."

Sam's name was called. She slowly walked forward, took the microphone and began to speak. One by one the insects bombarded her, and soon she was covered with shining, brown skinned beetles!

But Sam found it didn't matter any more. Happily she carried on preaching. God, who had called her to go to the nations, had made her equal to the challenge. The fear had gone, replaced by faith. God was the author and finisher of her faith. When He started something He always finished it.

The Father's Vision

Are you willing to be like a golf player ..?

ONCE you ask God to do what He wants in your life, His Holy
Spirit sets about leading and guiding you.

"Sam?"

"Yes Lord?"

"A man is going to contact you and ask you to speak at his church in Westminster, London. Please accept the invitation and I'll let you know what I would like you to do."

A few weeks later, a preacher asked Sam to speak one Sunday morning in his church. She travelled up to London, and sitting on the front row that morning, waiting to be invited to the platform, she had a vision. She was standing next to a man dressed in a cream shirt and khaki trousers. He was teaching her how to play golf. He was poised to hit the ball and slowly, with her by his side, he swung his club.

Then someone calling her name cut across her game of golf. Quickly opening her eyes, she remembered where she was and made her way to the platform. But as she looked at the congregation she found the vision of the game of golf hadn't gone away. Slowly she put her Bible away and pulling herself up to her full (not very tall) height she picked up the microphone.

"Are you willing to be like a golf player?" she said. "He emerges from the crowd and sturdily and carefully places his feet on solid ground. He places the ball between his feet and looks to see where he is going to hit it. With great concentration he swings and watches where the ball lands.

"Are you like the golfer who, after he has hit the ball, goes and looks for it, plants his feet solidly around it and begins the process again? Are you like the golfer focused intently on getting the ball into the last hole? Are you like a golf player who never gives up until the game is over?"

Sam became aware the congregation was listening intently.

"Have you asked Jesus to help you come out of the crowd, to be different from your friends? Have you asked Him to place your feet on solid ground and are you willing for Him to release His gifts and calling in your life? Have you asked Him to walk with you through the course of life, fulfilling His plans and purposes for you? Have you asked Him to give you wisdom and courage to complete the course He has laid out for you?

The congregation seemed stunned. One by one the people asked for prayer. Many, with tears in their eyes, began a relationship with a living Jesus.

"Father," Sam said, "thank you so much. I was going to preach on a different subject, but you showed me the vision of the golfer. How did you do that Lord? How did you know that was the subject the people needed to hear and not another one?"

"Sam, when people go to church or gather with friends and talk about me, I really want to meet with them. When two or three gather wanting to know me, I am right there. I take every opportunity to reveal who I am in ways they can understand. That is why I showed you the vision of the golf player. In that congregation were many people who played golf. I knew they would understand what you were saying. My Holy Spirit was speaking through you. I got their attention. That was why they wanted you to pray for them.

"I loved every minute of the meeting. I saw them. I knew them. I heard their prayers and drew near to them. That is why I asked the minister to invite you to share at his church. I knew you would preach what I gave you, on the spur of the moment. My Holy Spirit has been training you to 'see,' and then 'speak'."

"Wow," said Sam. "You are so aware of everyone's movements, Lord. You do exactly what you say you will. You don't lie, what you say, you carry out.

"Father, please look after all the people who were there. Show them your ways. Teach them your paths. Lead them in your truth, for you are the God of their salvation."

"Sam."

"Yes, Lord?"

"*Because* they received Jesus into their hearts, they *will* begin to walk in Him. Their faith *will* be rooted, built up and established in Him. They *will* continually abound with thanksgiving and my joy *will* flow out of them. The people in that congregation received a fresh impartation of my Holy Spirit. They *will* walk with me, talk with me and love me. I am so glad they went to that church that morning."

"Father," said Sam, "you are so lovely. You really do love the whole world! Please continue to send me and I will go."

The Father's Faithfulness

The healer of broken hearts ...

SOMETIMES Sam would look back at her life, and struggle with unhappy thoughts. If she took her mind off God and His love, she could easily start feeling very sorry for herself.

Sam grew up in an orphanage. Her mother was mentally ill, she never knew who her father was, and she didn't do well at school. To cope with the memories of her own history she had to allow God into her thoughts and let Him place His healing within her. He took her pains and griefs. Sam found He was the healer of the broken hearted; all she had to do was call on Him for His help.

Here is a poem she wrote, during that time.

The Wilderness

The wilderness is hard to take –
A ride that no one wants,
For when you get there, your heart is bare
And life is not a jaunt.
Scenes flood my mind, from far in time,
They stand and stare with one big glare
And say, "You're mine!"
My heart is still; life's lost its thrill –
It's time to reconcile.
All those pains and all those hurts –
"Will I one day smile?"

Amongst the busyness of life, I heard myself to say
"Will I draw near to my Saviour dear
And let Him show me the way?"
The challenge is on.
Where has He gone that I might find my friend?
I knew Him with me when I was young–
In fact He *was* my friend.

But today I looked ... to see the place
Where He alone had been.
And as I pondered that dear space
My heart cried out, "Where is your face?"

I saw His face more oft than not,
As He led me through the deep, deep troughs.
And if I fell or fainted nigh,
He'd reach down and lift me high.

The relationship I had with Him,
Was fun and fulfilling as life could be.
He knew me well, He held my hand,
And He led me into His promised plan.

But now my heart cries out to Him,
"Release me Lord from all my sin."
The mem'ries, the hurts of past years spent,
Have worn me out so I relent.
I cannot bear these sharp, sharp pains,
My heart and mind are far too strained.

Save me Lord this day I beg
So I may receive your daily bread –
The food and nourishment for my soul –
Your Spirit's power to make me whole.

I urgently pray this prayer today,
Because dear Lord you *are* the way,
To rid me of my pride and sin
And release your river deep within.

This wilderness is no fun place
I looked for mercy and I looked for grace.
But what I saw was far from this –
A place of sadness, a place of dread
A place with nowhere to lay my head.
Dry and barren, no place of retreat
Not my idea of sweet release.

But Lord this day I don't want to grumble,
For I know with you I can be humble.
If I just come to you and say,
"Lord, my Saviour have your way."

I know you will hear and with me reside
And lead me to your riverside.
That I may drink and have my fill
And learn to love you and be still.

The time will come Lord, this I know,
When these memory clouds will have to go.
But until then I will rest in you
knowing Lord you will see me through.

You won't leave me here an extra day
If it's not in your will or in your way.
So I ... trust you now and do my part
And leave you with my delicate heart.

Your hands reveal a father's care
And my heart, to you, I will lay bare.
This wilderness is not home for me
But knowing you're here, patient I'll be.

For you are my forever friend
And this dark night will have an end.
So, until then I say 'Thank you Lord'
And trust you Father, to send your word.

For your glory I pray. Amen"

It wasn't long before God came to Sam's side, picked her up and healed her memories of the past. She knew she was loved and He was good. The Bible says, "When you walk through the waters, He will be with you, or through the rivers, they will not overcome you. When you walk through the fire you shall not get burnt and the flame won't singe you." In other words, God will be there for you in every circumstance you find yourself in, because He is faithful and has promised never to leave you or forsake you. He loves you. Hang in there! Trust Him! He always keeps His promises.

The Father's Adventure

*Once you ask God to do what He wants
in your life, His Holy Spirit starts to take
you on adventures!*

"SAM?"

"Yes, Lord?"

"There are a couple of children in the United States who are wanting to be friends with me. Would you go over there and tell them about my love?"

"Yes, Lord. I'll go!" she said happily.

With an air ticket in hand, Sam left England and travelled to a children's camp in the USA. The camp was a girls' camp associated with Pioneer Girls of America. Wooden cabins dotted the hillside, and there were many secluded log cabins in the woods.

The organisers asked her to be a counsellor and care for ten campers each week.

One evening, a little eight-year-old girl named Bonnie gave her life to Jesus. The following evening another little girl, Gwen, wanted to do the same. But it had been a long day and Sam was tired. She told Gwen that she would pray for her the next day and the children snuggled into their beds ready for sleep.

After a few minutes Bonnie came to Sam's bedside. "Puffin (Sam's camp name), Gwen wants to make friends with Jesus. You can't pray for her tomorrow, she wants to be His friend tonight."

Sam turned to Bonnie and said with a smile, "Bonnie, why don't you pray with Gwen the way I prayed with you yesterday. You asked Jesus to take all your sins away and come into your life and He did." Bonnie looked at Sam and her eyes glinting with joy, ran to the end of the cabin and knelt down beside Gwen's bed. Sam heard their two quiet voices in the distance, and decided to see how things were going. She sat down gently on the end of Gwen's bed, listening.

The next minute, Bonnie banged Sam's leg with her hand. "Puffin! Puffin! What else can I say?" Sam gently prompted Bonnie in a prayer leading Gwen to Jesus as her friend and Saviour. Bonnie led her first person to Jesus at the age of eight.

The next morning, Gwen ran past the cabin. "Puffin," she shouted, "when I get to heaven and see Jesus would it be okay to give Him a hug?" Being British, Sam could have said, "Oh, just shake His hand. That'll do." But she didn't. She remembered what country she was in and shouted back, "Yes, He would love that!"

"Father" Sam said enthusiastically. "Gwen wanted to give you a hug and she couldn't even see you!"

"I know! My heart was jumping up and down with joy! I love it when my children love me! They don't have to see me; they just have to believe that I am there! When Gwen gets to heaven, I will be the first one to give her a hug!" He said with a father's smile.

"Wow! You are soooo lovely!" said Sam.

The Father's Joy

I am going to put a song in their hearts ...

I see three little boys in a church in Chicago, Sam. I would like you to meet them. Will you go to North America for me?"

"Father, you see everything," said Sam. "What's going to happen once I meet them?"

"Haha!" He said. "I am going to put a song in their hearts and I want you to hear it!"

"Sure, I'll go for you. Sounds fun."

It wasn't long before Sam was sitting with those three little boys, aged 8, 10 and 11. The main church service was being held upstairs, but Sam's task was to share the good news of Jesus with a group of little children, downstairs in the basement.

Once they were all seated Sam felt God's Holy Spirit come and settle upon them all. She knew God was with her. Very quickly she shared with the children Jesus' love, how the Son of God was crucified for their sins, buried, and rose again three days later. How Jesus had overcome sin and death, and was alive and wanted to be their friend.

Each child prayed and asked Jesus to come and live within them and take their sins away so they could be His friends. As He did this the room became very quiet. Suddenly one by one the boys began to laugh. Bernie, the oldest of the three boys, began to sing a song.

"For he's a jolly good fellow.
For he's a jolly good fellow!"

"Bernie! Bernie! "Who's a jolly good fellow?" said Sam with a big grin.

Bernie kept going, laughing.

"He's a jolly good fellow
which nobody can deny!"

"Bernie! Bernie! Is it Jesus? Is He a jolly good fellow because He died for you?" asked Sam in delight.

Bernie sang on.

"Nobody can deny! Nobody can deny!
He's a jolly good fellow
which nobody can deny!"

The joy of the Lord swept through that little room. The children laughed and sang and laughed some more! They nearly fell off their seats with God's joy. Their sins had been forgiven and now they were so happy. Friends with Jesus forever!

"Can we sing this in church on Sunday?" asked Bernie.

Sunday morning came and Bernie added more verses to his song.

He died on the cross for my sins.
He died on the cross for my sins.
He died on the cross for my sins,
which no one can deny!

He rose from the grave on the third day.
He rose from the grave on the third day.
He rose from the grave on the third day,
which no one can deny!

For He's a jolly good fellow!
For He's a jolly good fellow!
For He's a jolly good fellow,
which no one can deny!"

The congregation erupted with joy as the children sang their song.

"Sam!"

"Yes, Lord?"

"I couldn't stop laughing when you nearly fell off your seat. I loved it! When the children wanted me to become their friend, I was so happy! I came and made my home in their hearts, and I gave them my free gift of eternal life so they can be with me forever. I am so happy!

"Sam, thank you for leaving your family and friends and coming with me to Chicago. Thank you for being willing to say what I wanted you to say."

"That's OK Lord. You knew that song would make me laugh. It was hilarious. Did it really touch your heart?"

"Yes, because it came from their hearts, I loved it. From now on I will place my own song in them! They will have my song flowing through their veins! They will shout with joy to me and burst into singing! They will wake up in the morning singing my songs. They will be filled with my Holy Spirit, as they sing psalms, and hymns and spiritual songs! When they sing a love song to me, I will sing a love song to them! We will sing together!"

"Wow! Do you really sing songs over us?" asked Sam.

"Yes! I sing over you with joy and I fill people's hearts with my gladness!"

"Then Lord, please give me a song to worship you with. Just like Bernie. He didn't know what to sing but it was the right song for Him. I want to be like Bernie and not be ashamed to lift up my voice and praise you. Please put a song in my mouth and I will sing it from the rooftops."

"Wow! Then I will join you and together we will sing of all that I have done! Let's live in the beauty of holiness together!"

The Father smiled. He loved hearing Sam's voice, but now He was going to hear it in song! He couldn't wait!

Sam felt so loved. Her Father, Saviour and Friend was going to spend time with her as she sang a love song to Him, and He in turn was going to sing a love song back. What a relationship! What a friendship! She felt so secure in His love. She snuggled under the shadow of His wings!

The Father's Message

.. out of the corner of her eye she saw her right arm, then her left, travel right round to the back of the crowd

"SAM, there is a country where my children are suffering. They need encouragement. Will you go?"

"Lord, what would you like me to do there?"

"I would like you to deliver a message for me."

"Oh OK. If that is all you want me to do, I will do it."

Sam made her way to Pakistan. It was a comfort to think she was only going to deliver a message!

She flew into Lahore and stayed with a friend. After settling in, she was invited to attend a meeting.

Sam accepted the invitation, and began the three-hour journey.

"Is the meeting in a church?" she asked.

"No, out in a field," said her new friends.

"What sort of meeting is this?" she asked two hours later.

"It's an evangelistic rally."

Twenty minutes from the venue Sam asked the final question, "Who is the speaker?"

"Oh, you are!"

"Me?" she shouted, pointing to herself. In complete shock she struggled to hear what God might be wanting to say.

Entering the city she saw posters on the walls, "Evangelist coming! Bring the sick and let God heal them!" She couldn't believe her eyes.

"Father, you said I was coming here to deliver a message. I delivered the letter I was given, but I never knew you were talking about this! I need your help! Please put your words in my mouth!"

Six hundred people from all walks of life, waited in the field for Sam to speak. Thirty men sat on the platform. Sam squeezed into the middle – only to learn there had been a death threat from a local radical group. As she realised what that might mean and saw the police marksmen on the rooftops she heard her name being called. It was her time to speak. She lowered her head down to the microphone.

Just then, out of the corner of her eye, she saw her right arm begin to extend and travel around the crowd to the back. As she looked at it, she saw her other arm do the same thing! Then her hands grasped each other and she saw herself drawing the crowd towards the microphone. "Jesus loves you," she said. "He will never hurt you. He died on the cross for your sins. He rose again and is alive today. If you want to get to know Him pray this prayer with me, 'Lord Jesus, please forgive my sins and come into my heart. I give you my life. Be my Lord and Saviour.'"

When the interpreter had finished and the crowd had finished praying, there was a enormous eruption of cheering and clapping.

"What's happening?" said Sam in shock, looking at the interpreter.

"Hundreds have just made friends with Jesus," she replied.

Astonished, Sam stared about her.

"Lord, I was willing to deliver a message for you, but I never knew you had this in mind – standing before all these people," Sam protested.

"If I told you what I had planned, you would never have gone," God said soothingly. "I cared for you. I was by your side all the time. I gave you words to say and eyes to see. I knew you would share with them what I wanted. I knew you would be ready to speak for me anytime, anywhere, regardless of the circumstances. I know it was such a surprise but I knew you were the right person for the occasion.

"Sam, if you had not gone, how would I have been able to love and forgive all those people who needed me. If no one goes to preach, how can they get saved? Thank you so much for going," He said reassuringly.

Seeing all those people respond to His love, Sam realised God was right. He did know she would go. He knew that if He gave her a vision she would share it. Yes, He was with her all the time, protecting her. He was full of surprises! He had won the day. Hundreds of people had now become His friends. Sam began to relax.

"Father, I am so glad you know all about me. You know when I sit down and when I stand up, when I am well, or sick. You are with me all the time. It's true, if no one goes and tells the people about your love and forgiveness how will they know you. You are a true friend. Jesus, please forgive me for being grumpy. I love you!" she said happily.

The Father's Promise

Because you put me first
I will give you everything else to enjoy ...

"SAM, I would like you to go to Kenya. In the first week I want to teach you something beautiful about me. Will you go?"

Sam, intrigued, responded with delight, "Yes, Lord."

But she also added some conditions. "Father, you can send me to Kenya, but I don't want to be a tourist. I have heard that there are many sandy beaches and lovely hotels in Kenya. Please don't send me there. Send me out to the countryside and put me somewhere that matters to you. I want to go straight from the airport to the bush."

The Father scratched His chin. He knew what He had planned, but wanted it to be a surprise, so He quietly watched as her journey unfolded.

It wasn't long before Sam's flight landed in Nairobi. The leaders of a children's mission met her, but instead of travelling 20 miles out of the city, to an orphanage and school, she found herself on a slow train to Mombasa – the tourist capital of Kenya.

As Sam lay on the beach, with palm trees and coconuts surrounding her, she prayed.

"Father?"

"Yes, Sam?"

"Before I came to Kenya I asked you to not let me be a tourist."

" Yes, I know."

"Why then am I lying on a beach, with palm trees and coconuts all around me. The sun is shining, and I am living the life of a tourist?"

"Sam! Because you put me and my work first in your life, I decided to give you everything else to enjoy!"

" Wow! You mean if I give you my life and get to know you and ask you to lead me, you will surprise me with things like this?"

"Yes! If you lose your life for my sake you will find it. I will give you life, full to overflowing! I have so many things in store for you! I want you to enjoy following me. Because you have my peace and joy, you are a carrier of my presence. Everywhere you go, I go! When you get on a plane, I am with you. I will not leave you alone or let you be lonely; I am your companion.

"If you want to run your own life, and do your own thing, the life I want to give you cannot come to pass. If you live with me and for me, all these other blessings will be yours as well. So you need never worry about tomorrow, for tomorrow will look after itself. I am your provider. I am now, and I always will be!"

"Father, you are my all in all! Thank you so much for having your eye on the sparrow, and also on me!" said Sam.

Years later, Sam went on a cruise ship to Norway. She enjoyed it very much. Towards the end of the week, sitting on the top deck looking at the peaceful reflection of the boat in the water below, she said, "Lord, is there any way I can do this each year? It is so lovely and restful."

"Sam, of course you can do it each year. I have told you before, if you put me first in your life, I will give you everything else to enjoy!"

So – no surprise! For the following four years Sam and her friends were given opportunities to minister on cruise ships. As usual, what God said, He did.

The Father's Hand

I would like Jesus
to hold my hand now and forever ...

"SAM, there is a little church down by the Black Sea and a lady is going there for the first time. I want you to introduce her to me."

Sam heard His still small voice again. "Yes, Lord. Here I am, send me," she said.

Sam flew from England to Bulgaria, was taken down to a town on the Black Sea and asked to preach on a Sunday morning. That morning the church was very full and many people were standing. During the service, a woman entered – a gypsy. She pushed her way forward to the front row and seeing an empty chair, sat on it. Sitting at the back of the church, Sam smiled. She knew this woman was not familiar with church meetings, so she kept a close eye on her.

Soon it was time for Sam to preach. She walked past the lady, and up to the platform. While she was speaking Sam noticed the woman staring at her intently. She was listening closely.

The meeting ended, and people clustered round Sam, asking her to pray for them. The gypsy woman was among them. "Please will you pray for me?" she said. Lifting her hand above her head and with determination in her voice, she cried, "I would like Jesus to hold my hand now and forever." With tears in her eyes, Sam reached out for the woman's hand, lifted it upwards and prayed, "Father, hear the cry of this lady's heart. Please hold her hand now and forever."

God's peace and stillness settled upon them like a thick blanket. He had heard her cry. The sadness left her eyes. Hope had come. She could live knowing that her Heavenly Father had heard her cry. She had drawn near to Him, and He had drawn near to her. She had placed her hand in His and He had placed His hand in hers. The gypsy woman smiled, God smiled and Sam smiled!

"Father, wasn't that wonderful! You reached out and held her hand!"

"Yes, Sam. Of course. My hand is not so short that it cannot save, or my ear so deaf that it cannot hear! I heard her cry. I rescued her! I love her." Sam heard the smile in His voice.

The Father's Surprise

Father, you even notice the sparrows ...

"SAM? Are you ready for another adventure?"

"Father, wherever you send me, it's always an adventure," said Sam enthusiastically. "You are so full of life! You know everything, see everything and want to help in every situation! Yes, I am ready for another adventure!"

"Thank you Sam! I have seen a man who is very sad. He lives in England, but his wife has recently died, and he is travelling back to the place where they had their honeymoon. Will you please go to Myanmar (Burma) for me? I need someone to be there at the right time, and in the right place. I will show you this man."

"Father, you even notice the sparrows, and your eye is on every person you have created. If he needs your help Lord, then of course, I will go. Please help me be sensitive to your leading. Thank you Father."

Sam prepared for the journey. If her Heavenly Father wanted to help this man she had to go, so it wasn't long before she arrived in Myanmar, and settled into her hotel.

She had also been asked to speak to some church leaders and Sunday School teachers.

One morning, Sam and her fellow worker, walked down the stairs to the busy hotel restaurant. It was 8.30am and time for breakfast. They had a full teaching schedule that day, and their minds were on their lessons.

As they were talking Sam was aware of God's presence. She raised her head and, in the spirit, saw a man walk through the restaurant towards the checkout, pay his bill, stop, turn around and come and sit at their table! Sam quickly whispered to her friend, "Pauline, there's a man over there who is going to head towards the checkout, then turn around and come over to sit with us!"

Pauline looked at Sam. "No way!"

A few minutes went by. Sam, watching and eating, kept her eye on the man. Sure enough, when the time came, he paid his bill, walked towards the exit door, stopped, looked around and came towards their table!

Sam and Pauline were so astonished they could barely contain themselves! The man introduced himself, pulled up a chair and began to unburden his heart. His wife had recently died and he had travelled back to the hotel where they had spent their honeymoon.

"Why did God let my wife die?" he asked tearfully.

For the next hour Sam and Pauline helped the man work through his grief. He had travelled from a town in England that was only three miles from Sam's home address!

God knew that Sam and her friend would understand his culture and language, and that Pauline, a church minister, would be able to share God's compassion and love for him during his loss.

The man began to receive God's love. "Cast all your cares upon Him because He cares for you," the Bible says. As the man did this God's peace flooded his heart.

"Father, you are incredible," gushed Sam. "I know you say that we are to pray that the Lord of the harvest would send labourers into His harvest, because it is so abundant and there aren't enough labourers, but Lord, you sent me all the way to Burma, to open my eyes to see this man. Wow! How did you show me this man coming to my table, when he hadn't even paid his bill?"

"Well, I am eternal! I live in the past, present and future. I just needed to open your eyes so you could see what I was seeing. I wanted to prepare you. You should have seen your faces when John sat at your table. I laughed and laughed! I love it when I can supernaturally reveal my purposes to my children. You will be surprised what I can do. If you look for me with all your heart you will find me. I will open your eyes and you will see more and more!"

"Wow! You are full of surprises!"

"Yes, I am! Can I send you somewhere else?"

"Father, how can you surprise me more than this? This adventure was incredible!"

"Aha! Wait and see! I am enjoying every minute of this! I love leading you, and teaching you. As time goes by, you will get to know my thoughts and my nature. That is why I call you my friend! I tell my secrets to my friends. I am changing you all the time, so that you love to do what pleases me. Enjoy my leadings. Enjoy my plans, for they bring peace and not harm. They lead to your future and wonderful hope. Enjoy my love for you!"

Sam smiled. What else could she do?

The Father's Word

*You will tell the mountain to move
and it will move ...*

"SAM, I can hear the cries of my people. There is great pain. They are being killed and injured because they believe in me. Will you go to Nigeria and tell them I have heard their cries and am sending people to help them?

Sam thought very hard. God had asked her to go to a country at war. Christians were being killed, God's people – her family!

"Yes Lord. Send me. I will go for you."

"You will come across mountains you cannot go through or around. But you will tell the mountain to move and it will. I will strengthen your faith. I will also open your eyes. You will see what you have never seen before. I will give you courage. Be bold! Don't shrink back. Just trust me," He said encouragingly.

Sam knew this assignment would be different from any other. What did the Father have in store for her? she wondered.

Four weeks before Sam's arrival, 3,000 people had been killed in religious riots. Many of them had loved Jesus and had lost their lives.

Arriving in Nigeria, she saw a newspaper article showing a photo of a Baptist minister sitting in a hospital bed holding up half of his right arm. It quoted the pastor, "I only gave my arm for Jesus. I wish I could have given Him my life." Six other Baptist ministers were killed during the riots, but this particular minister lived to tell the tale.

Sam was asked to help train Sunday School workers. This meant travelling to a northern town, Sokoto, on the Niger border, not far from where the rioting had taken place, to hold training seminars for teachers.

With her Nigerian friend and 20 other passengers, Sam boarded the bus. Squawking chickens were tied to a post near their feet and packets of food and car tyres were stuffed into the aisles. It was 5.30 am as the laden bus began its long journey northwards.

Eight hours later, the bus abruptly stopped. Immigration officials near the Niger border boarded the bus and asked for their papers.

"Passports! Passports!" shouted a man in a blue uniform as he threaded his way down the overcrowded isle to the back of the bus, to Sam and her co-worker.

"I've left mine with friends in the city we've just left," said Sam.

"Off the bus!" he shouted, gesturing with his thumb. Sam and her friend clambered over the chickens and tyres to the front of the bus, dismounted and quickly looked around. A large crowd had gathered. Immigration officials dressed in brown and blue uniforms walked towards them. Other men in long silky robes and round hats joined the crowd. The bus had stopped in the middle of nowhere.

"Where are your passports and ID cards?" asked a tough looking official.

"I left my passport with friends in a city we've passed through earlier," she repeated.

"You're lying. You don't have a passport. You are trying to enter our country as an illegal immigrant. We will deport you back to England this evening!"

Sam didn't know whether to laugh or cry. She thought about saying, "Thank you," but didn't. She just stared at the official in disbelief. Then she heard another official shout at the bus driver.

"Get these ladies' belongings off the bus. They are going nowhere."

The driver and his passengers surrounded the immigration official. Locking eyes with him the driver retorted, "No, I am not going anywhere without these ladies. They are my passengers!" And with that he stubbornly folded his arms.

The official shouted at him once more, "Get these ladies' things off the bus!"

But the crowd refused to budge. The official began to get very angry. No one was following his orders, so he went back to where the women were standing and joined his other colleagues.

His assistant began to ask Sam's friend questions. "What job do you do?"

"I work with Children's Evangelism Ministry," she said.

"Children's what?" shouted the man. "Did you say Children's Education Ministry? "

"No. Children's Evangelism Ministry," she replied.

Another official turned to Sam, "Ah, so that's what you are. You are an evangelist!"

Sam was about to say "Yes," when suddenly in the corner of her eye, she saw the word 'evangelist' stretched out in front of her in black and white. The letters were wriggling! God was warning her. "Sam! Sam! There is something wrong with that word, don't use it." (What Sam didn't know at the time was that just the day before, all international evangelists had been banned from entering the country.)

She replied, "I am a children's worker, visiting children in third world countries."

"Children's worker! Children's worker! What's a children's worker?" yelled the official.

At this point the whole crowd became silent. Sam was so frightened that tears flowed down her cheeks. "Lord, what's a children's worker? Help me!" she begged.

Then the words the Lord had spoken to her before the journey came to mind. "You will come across mountains you cannot go through or around. You will say to the mountain, "Be removed!" and it will be." Sam's tears cleared, the crowd stared and with the little faith she had, she whispered, "Mountain, go!"

Immediately, the head official began to shout and wave his arms. "You men, move away from these girls." As the crowd parted, the girls were asked to walk up a hill toward the official's office. Five minutes later, a voice shouted from behind, "Stand still!" They stood still and turned around. One of the men put his finger in Sam's face and said angrily, "You stay right here. We'll be back!"

As they walked towards the office, Sam and her co-worker were left alone for the first time and a funny thought came to Sam. She remembered a few weeks earlier, before flying to Nigeria, her church leader had given her an audio cassette. It was titled, "We Don't Give God a Chance to Send Angels." Now, this would be a great time for God to send angels! A big smile spread across her face. As she watched the backs of the departing men she prayed, "Father, I ask for two angels to go with those men, and Holy Spirit, you go with them also, and tell them what God's plans are for my future. Do I go back to England or carry on with my travels to Sokoto?"

Fifteen minutes passed and not a word could be heard anywhere. It seemed that even the camels nearby had stopped shuffling, the cars had stopped running, and everyone had stopped talking. Everything waited quietly. Eventually the men came out of their office and strolled over to them.

"Sam, are you going to laugh or cry?" said a little official, pointing his finger in her face.

By this time Sam wasn't very feeling very communicative.

"You tell me what you are going to tell me, and I will tell you if I want to laugh or cry," she replied.

"I believe you are on God's business. Go!"

Tears came to Sam's eyes.

"I believe you are on God's business. Go!" he shouted again.

Sam quickly turned to her friend. "Let's go!" They rapidly made their way down the hill and walked through the crowd back onto the bus. It was so quiet you could have heard a pin drop. The passengers reboarded and the bus began to cough its way along the road to Sokoto, their final destination.

Ten minutes later her friend whispered, "We have just seen a miracle. That man doesn't know what came out of his mouth!" For the remaining two hours they sat in silence, trying to take in all that had happened.

In Sokoto, the passengers were very kind. They helped Sam and her friend unload their suitcases into two wheelbarrows, and pushed them to their next stop, the taxi rank. From there they were driven to the Baptist church and the teachers' training program.

For three days Sam shared God's love with the teachers. She encouraged them to tell the children in the villages that Jesus loved them and was watching over them. As God's children they could safely trust Him with all their hearts. As she spoke, the teachers' confidence and courage grew. They wanted to go and share Jesus' love with everyone they met! Even though people were being killed for talking about Jesus in that area, they knew God would encourage and strengthen them.

"Don't give up on your friendship with Jesus," Sam urged the teachers, "He is worth living for, and dying for! Those who give their lives for Him will find life, but those who withhold their lives will lose them."

She prayed for many people. Some had walked three days to get to the training seminars. She placed each one into God's care and with the seminars over, said her farewells and made her way back to the south.

Still without her passport, she prepared herself for a repeat performance at the border. As the taxi crept to the barrier, three men dressed in blue and brown uniforms came running over and Sam braced herself.

"We are so glad to see you again. We trust you have had a very good time in Sokoto? You can go through the border. Enjoy the rest of your stay in Nigeria!"

Sam was astounded. So astounded she didn't even open her mouth.

As she passed through the border, Sam turned and looked out of the back window. "Lord, why were those men so nice to me? I didn't have my passport. They could have deported me."

"Well, you know that when I begin a work, I finish it! I took you through the border, don't you think I'd be able to bring you back?"

Looking up to heaven, Sam smiled quietly. "Yes, you are able," she said, and as her smile widened she whispered, "Thank you."

"You will come across mountains you cannot go through or go round. But you will say to the mountain be removed and it will be. I will strengthen your faith. I will also open your eyes. You will see what you have never seen before. I will give you courage. Be bold! Do not shrink back. Just trust me!" He said reassuringly.

As Sam turned over in her mind what He had promised, gratitude and adoration gushed up. He had done everything He had promised. He was so faithful.

"Thank you, Father" she said, her heart bursting. "You always tell the truth. You knew everything that was going to happen. You saw what I didn't see. You were ahead of me all the way. You changed the minds of those officials. You are very powerful, Lord. No one is greater than you. You gave me courage when I was quaking and telling the mountain to go! When I was so weak you were strong! You opened my eyes and warned me when I saw the word, 'evangelist' wiggling! You prompted me with the right words. You were there speaking through me. You were not slow to help me! Thank you Father for loving me! Thank you!"

"Sam, thank you for thanking me! I love to hear your voice! Whenever I hear it I want to draw close to you, because your heart is true and honest and you want to be close to me. Thank you for loving me. You can talk to me at any time because I am with you. I will be there. I will never go away. My ear is always open to you. Speak to me and I will answer. I am for you and not against you, I love you!"

Sam was overwhelmed by the Lord's love for her. In the stillness of His presence her heart responded, "Speak Lord, for I love hearing your voice."

The Father's Heart

Do you think Jesus will remember me..?

"SAM, there is a little boy in the United States I long to make my friend, but only if he wants to. Would you go over to the USA and let him know about my love? I will show you where to go and what to say. I will help you."

Sam had been visiting many nations sharing God's love with everyone she met, and now God had another assignment for her.

"Yes, Lord. I will go."

This time Sam went to Alabama, in the United States, and was invited to speak to a Boys' Brigade troop. Sixteen boys about ten years old gathered in a church hall for a Bible study. As they sat in a circle on the floor, Sam began to share the story of Jesus dying on the cross. With a piece of paper in hand, she folded it, and cut it in a special way. Three crosses appeared. Placing them on the floor, she explained that the cross in the middle represented Jesus, God's Son, who had died to set us free. The other two crosses represented two thieves, who were being crucified at the same time.

One of the thieves looked over to Jesus.

"Jesus remember me when you begin to reign forever," he pleaded.

With love in His eyes Jesus turned to the man, "Today you will be with me in Paradise," He promised.

But the other thief didn't want to talk to Jesus.

As Sam turned his cross over, to illustrate that the thief's heart had turned away from Jesus, God's Holy Spirit began to speak to one of the boys.

At a church service the following day the boy stopped Sam in the hallway. "I have been thinking about the story," he said. "I don't want to be like the thief who turned away from Jesus. I want to be like the one who said, 'Jesus remember me when you come into your kingdom.' He looked seriously into Sam's eyes, "Do you think Jesus would remember me?"

Sam smiled. "If you would like Him to, I am sure He would."

Standing in the hallway, with people passing, he closed his eyes, and lifting up his head, cried out, "Jesus, please remember me." He paused, and awareness of God's love seemed to explode inside him. He gave Sam a long, wide-eyed look, then a brilliant smile, and shot off down the corridor.

As Sam watched him go, she smiled. "Father, you saw that little boy didn't you? You knew he wanted to get to know you!"

"Sam, I was just longing to put my love and joy into his heart, but I had to wait for him to ask me. I was so excited when I saw him lift his face to me. The minute he spoke to me, I placed my joy, love, and forgiveness within him. His heart has now become my home. He is at peace with me, and I am at peace with him. My peace is eternal. I am so happy!"

"Oh Father, I am so glad you're happy! May every child in the world get to know you! May they know that you are alive and care for them. Thank you so much for sending me on your special adventures! You know what is best for my life. I don't want to plan my future – you be my future! Thank you so much Father!"

The Father's Persistence

*... when just one person comes to
Jesus the angels rejoice*

"SAM, can I send you to Ghana? There is a little boy who wants
to get to know me, but he needs someone to tell him. Will you go
for me?"

"Yes, Lord. Of course I will go."

Her assignment in Ghana was to teach Sunday School leaders.

During one of the evening seminars there was a power failure, so Sam attached two candles to the pulpit. Looking up at her audience all she could see in the flickering candlelight were their flashing white teeth, ruddy cheeks and the whites of their eyes. She was about to start speaking when the Lord interrupted her. "I want you to ask for testimonies."

"But Father, there is no point in asking for testimonies. It's too early. I'm only teaching at this stage."

But God persisted! So Sam agreed to co-operate.

"Does anyone have anything to share?" she asked.

A boy of ten years, walked up to the pulpit, and looked closely at Sam.

"Yesterday, I came to your meeting," he said. "Last night, I went to bed and talked to God. Then I sang to Him. Suddenly He spoke to me, and said that if I wanted to make friends with Him, I had to come tonight and ask the white lady to introduce me to Him!"

Sam was stunned. In front of the teachers, she introduced George to Jesus and he received Jesus' love and forgiveness. Joy filled his heart and he was born into God's family, forever to be with Jesus who loved him and gave His life for him.

The Bible says that when one person comes to Jesus and turns away from their sin, the angels rejoice in heaven! That evening there was great rejoicing in heaven!

"Father?"

"Yes, Sam?"

"Do you know everything about every child in the world?"

"Yes, Sam! My eyes saw them before they were born! I was there while they were being formed in their mothers' wombs. I knew what they were going to look like and who their parents were going to be. I know when they are going to stand up and sit down. I am always with them. In fact, I have assigned an angel to every child."

"Is that why, when you saw George lying on his bed singing and praying, you spoke to him and asked him to come to the meeting tonight?"

"Yes, his angel came before me. I saw George wanted to know me, so I arranged that you would be there and introduce him to me. I made it possible for you to travel to Ghana. I met your costs as you put your trust in me. Nothing is impossible to those who believe!"

"Wow! Father. Thank you so much!"

The Father's Encouragement

... they are my silver and gold

"SAM! Are you still available? I want to send you to another country?"

"Yes, Lord!" said Sam smiling.

"Father, you *know* I am available. If a nation makes you sad you know I will go," said Sam, not knowing what this next assignment would bring.

"I would like to send you to Indonesia – a group of islands near Singapore. Would you tell the people I love them and want to be their friend?"

Sam packed her bags and travelled to Indonesia from one island to another bringing God's love to the people.

Flying over the islands one day chatting to God, Sam reminded Him that Indonesia was a Moslem nation. She was surprised to hear Him whisper, "No, it's not!"

"Yes, it is!" she said.

"No, it's not," the Lord repeated.

"Lord, the media says it is. If it's not, then what is it?"

"It is my silver and gold!"

"Your silver and gold? What do you mean?" she said.

"When I look at the nations, I don't see what most people see. I see my people. I see the ones I created. I see myself loving and forgiving them. I became the Lamb that was sacrificed for them. I see people in all nations accepting me, turning to me and following me.

"Many did that in Indonesia, and made me their friend! My life and love radiated through them. Some were shamed or killed for knowing me. I too was shamed and killed – I felt their pain. But I overcame death and have the keys of death and Hell! My children, who lost their lives for my sake, are now safe in my hands. They are my silver and gold! That's why, when I look over Indonesia I see my children, not those who hate me, but those who love me! They are my silver and gold – precious jewels! When their life here is over, I gather my jewels to myself and they will be with me forever."

"Father, thank you for sending me among your silver and gold. Let your light shine through me, so I reflect your glory! May the people see it and be glad! Let them know that there is a Heavenly Father calling their name! Draw them to yourself. Thank you Father for your encouragement!" said Sam.

The Father's Language

*... it sounded like a freight train
coming through the tunnel !*

"SAM, would you go to North Carolina for me? There are many children there wanting to know my presence and power. Will you go and tell them about me, please?"

"Father, I know you love children and if these children are on your heart today, I will go. Thank you Father."

Sam was asked to speak to some children at a family conference. While their parents were upstairs, she spent time with the children downstairs.

After the children left the first session, Sam and her co-worker stayed behind to pray. They thanked God for what He had done in the children's lives that morning and asked Him what He would like to do for them in the evening.

Just as they had finished praying Sam looked around the room. About three feet off the ground she saw lots of little white dots of light.

"Can you see those little white lights," she asked her friend.

"No," she said.

Sam realised God was trying to tell her something important.

"Lord, where are there lights in the Bible?" asked Sam.

She started in Genesis and went through to Revelation to see if she could remember any story that mentioned bright lights. The only bright lights she could think of were the Holy Spirit's tongues of fire that descended on the disciples' heads on the Day of Pentecost!

"That's it," she thought to herself. "That is the story I am going to speak on tonight. God is going to fill all the children with His Holy Spirit!" Exciting!

So many children attended the meeting that furniture had to be removed to make room for them. Once they were all seated on the floor, Sam noticed that their heads were approximately three feet off the ground. She knew something very special was going to happen to the children that evening.

The children listened intently as Sam explained the story of Pentecost. At the end they crouched on the floor, tucked their heads between their knees and thanked God for what He had taught them.

Walking between them, Sam placed her hands on each head and asked for the Holy Spirit to come and fill them with His power. It wasn't long before she heard what she thought was the sound of a freight train coming through a tunnel! Bewildered for a moment, it didn't take her long to realise that the noise was coming from the children. With their heads so close to the floor their voices sounded like a loud rumble. They were speaking in tongues – just as the disciples did on the Day of Pentecost. God had filled them with His Holy Spirit, and now they were speaking in new languages as the Spirit helped them!

Sam was astonished! Twenty children, praying in unknown tongues as loud as they could. What a noise! It was amazing! As they quietened down, the children became so overwhelmed by the love of Jesus that they began to cry tears of joy. As they thanked Him the peace of God filled the room.

"Father?"

"Yes, Sam."

"Wow! Did you see that? You filled all those children with your Holy Spirit. You helped them speak in languages they had never learned! You're amazing! How did you do that?"

"Sam! If only two or three people get together I am there with them! You had 20 children and not just them, but me and their angels as well! I have assigned an angel to each child to walk alongside them and help them.

"When you laid your hands on them to receive my presence and power I breathed upon them and they received my Spirit. He is like a river inside them. When He was released He gave them words to speak that they had never heard before. Sometimes they are earthly languages, sometimes angels' languages.

"When they speak in tongues they speak mysteries to me! But because they are speaking a heavenly language that comes from me they say the things I love to hear. Sometimes, if they pray in tongues with other people nearby, I give those people the interpretation in their own earthly language!"

"Lord, everyone in the room received your gift. Can anyone receive your power?"

"Sam, whoever draws near to me I will not send away. I have no favourites. If you want to be close to me I will come close to you – it's as simple as that! The ones who *really* want to be close get to know me and I get to know them.

"Can you imagine that a father would give his son a stone to eat if he asked his dad for a piece of bread, or a snake if he asked for some fish. It's the same with me and my children. I only give good gifts. So whoever asks for my Holy Spirit and power, will receive my Spirit and power, because I love to give good gifts to my children."

"Wow! Father, that's incredible! We ask, and then receive. Thank you for sending me to the children to see you bless them. They cried with joy because they caught a glimpse of how much you loved them! Strengthen them with your power so that they will never forget how good you are!"

"Sam, as I said before, if you acknowledge me in all you do I will always lead you. Trust me completely and don't try to work everything out yourself. Take big gulps of me because I taste so good. And, as you know, my compassion for you will never ever end!"

"Yes, Lord," said Sam looking up at her Heavenly Father, wide-eyed with a big smile on her face. "You're so amazing!"

The Father's Invitation

*"Lord," Sam said uncertainly, "India is a hot
country and they eat curry, very hot curry ...*

"SAM, would you go to India and pick up my children and put
them into my hands?"

"India?!

"Yes India!"

Sam knew how much the Lord loved children so she was very careful how she phrased her response.

"Lord," she said uncertainly, "India is a hot country and they wear very different clothes from me. They speak a very different language and eat curry, very hot curry!" she said.

"I know," He said smiling. "But I gave my life for them. Please will you go over to India. I want the children to hear about my love.

"There is a big harvest but not many workers," He added. There seemed to be an ache in the Lord's voice.

Reflecting on God's love for children in India, there was only one response Sam knew how to make. "Yes, Lord. Yes, I will go for you! Give me your message and I will pick up your children and place them in your hands."

As she agreed to go a deep peace filled her – and joy. She knew she had made the right decision. She didn't know what was ahead but she knew she could trust Him with all of it.

So – another air ticket in hand and this time, India.

Travelling with a ministry team from Mexico to help her, Sam began to mull over what the Lord had said. "He wants me to put the Indian children into His hands. How do I do that?" she asked herself. Having no idea at all, she leaned back in her seat, closed her eyes and dozed off. Worrying about the future was not going to help. Sam gave all her tomorrows to God knowing they were all in His care.

On arrival, she booked herself into a hotel in the city of Visak, and there, standing by the front door, was a little Indian boy. But this child wasn't like any she had seen. A wide orange glow was sitting on his shoulders and hovering over his head!

As Sam stood and stared, the boy froze! He didn't move, she didn't move! They just stared at each other. It was as if time had stood still. "Lord, what am I seeing?" Sam asked. A few seconds passed. The boy relaxed, turned, and ran away. Wondering if she was daydreaming, Sam picked up her suitcases and made her way to her room.

The next evening Sam and the Mexican ministry team were invited to join an evangelistic rally in the local city park. It was a night-time event and thousands of people had gathered. Sitting on the front row in the sweltering heat, batting away flies Sam listened to what the evangelist was saying.

"Jesus loves you! He gave His life for you! Make friends with Him! He is alive!"

People began to raise their hands wanting to give their lives to Jesus. As the rally went on more and more people responded to the preacher's invitation to trust God for all their needs. Many were sick. Some came with walking sticks and in wheelchairs, but when the man of God asked Jesus to heal them, they threw their walking sticks away and stepped out of their wheelchairs, and began to run around the platform shouting for joy! Jesus had healed them! Wow!

The following evening Sam and the Mexicans were invited by a team of Indian Christians for a meal at the hotel – and there he was again, the little Indian boy she had seen on her arrival. The boy stopped and stared. Sam, looked closely at him, realising there had to be something special about him.

Slowly she went over to him and asked if she could pray for him. He looked at her and then ran through the restaurant to a tall man standing in the far corner. As they began whispering to each other, she recognised the man the little boy was talking to. It was the evangelist who had spoken to the big crowd the night before!

The boy quietly made his way back to Sam and stood in front of her, head bowed. Sam placed her hands gently on his head and began to pray, "Please Lord, this little boy needs to know you. Fill him with your presence and power. Let him live for you. Be with him!" After the prayer the boy quickly ran back to his family.

Next morning, at the breakfast table, Sam suddenly found a big hand placed right in front of her nose. It belonged to the evangelist – the one who had been preaching to 25,000 people in the park the night before! While her heart began to beat wildly, the man gestured towards another table and asked if she would sit with his family.

Picking up her bag, Sam joined the man's wife and their small boy. Again her attention was drawn to the little boy. "Sir," she said to the evangelist, "your son is very aware of God. If you don't let him share this with others now, he will lose it and you will have to ask God to give it back to him when he's a teenager!"

His eyes wide, the boy's father leaned gently across the table towards his eight-year-old son. "Son, would you like to pray for the people on Monday night?" The little boy nodded in agreement.

Breakfast over, Sam packed her bags. It was time to say goodbye to the nation of India and get to the airport.

On the flight home she remembered God's invitation to her, "Will you go to India and pick up my children and place them into my hands?" She thanked the Lord for His invitation. She had only prayed for one little eight year old boy but she was so glad she had been able to.

It wasn't long before Sam heard what had happened when the evangelist's son prayed for the people that Monday night. Never in India's history had there been such a move of God among children as there was that night, the evangelist reported.

About 40,000 people had gathered in the city park, on the final evening. The small boy went to the microphone and prayed, "Lord, heal all the babies who are sick! Forgive the sins of the people and bring the presence of God to this city of Visak!" As he prayed people began to weep. His father, seeing what was happening, took the microphone and asked all children 15 years old and under to stand up. Hundreds of teenagers rose to their feet.

"Jesus loves you," he went on. "He gave His life for you! He died for you. Will you love Him? Will you give your life to Him? He is here now! Speak to Him."

The children talked to God. They gave their sins to Jesus and received His forgiveness. The Holy Spirit came to live within them. They became God's children and He became their father! A new relationship began and heavenly joy entered their lives.

The speaker invited children who had encountered Jesus to come up to the platform and describe what had happened. One child said that he saw Jesus beckoning him to follow. Other children told their stories.

"Can you go to India and pick up my children and put them into my hands?" the Father had asked Sam. He knew all about that little boy, and the faith he would have to speak to a big crowd. God knew he'd be in that particular hotel at exactly the time Sam arrived and that Sam would see the orange glow on his head and shoulders, meet him again in the restaurant, meet his family and be involved in setting the boy apart for God.

Through one little boy hundreds of children in India made friends with Jesus that night.

Father, thank you so much for letting me see your presence and power.

The Father's Assignment

Sam, will you go to Russia for me?

"SAM, one of my children needs help. He doesn't know he needs it, but when he does, I want you to be there to help him. Will you go to Russia for me?"

"Russia this time?"

"Yes, Russia!"

Sam smiled, "Yes," she said without hesitation. Another adventure – destination probably Siberia.

On the train to Siberia, Sam and her friend Heather found they were travelling with a team of 27 young American Christians planning to perform evangelistic street theatre in a another city near the Ural Mountains – closer than where Sam was going.

But an official announcement three days into the journey threw Sam's plans into disarray. Their onward train travel into Siberia was suddenly delayed and no one knew for how long. Their only option was to join the American team. Permission granted, they headed for the city and booked into a hotel.

The following day, the American group walked around the town handing out leaflets advertising the event the following day. With only two days to go before they had to be travelling back home Sam and Heather wondered what the Lord had in mind.

They weren't left to wonder for long.

During the night, the leader of the American team came down with food poisoning and early the next morning there was a knock on Sam's door. "Steven's sick. He wants to know if you would take over the leadership of the team."

Quickly Sam and Heather left for the centre of town. In a large white tent, 50 American and Russian young people were gathering for a morning Bible study. Knowing Steven had asked Sam to stand in for him, the team asked her to lead the Bible study.

"Bible, a Bible! Has anyone got a Bible?" Sam whispered urgently. Someone passed a Bible along the row of chairs to where Sam was sitting. Opening it up she began to preach. It was 7.30am.

And so it continued. Before the day was out Sam had preached in the public square and led the team through the day's events.

The following day, she and Heather found their way back to the train station, to begin their journey home.

"Father, thank you for sending me to Russia! You knew Steven wasn't going to be well. How did you get me to take his place? He didn't even know me. He had only met me two days earlier."

"Sam! When I train someone and grant them my gifts, I know exactly when, where, and how to bring them to the forefront.

"I had already whispered to Steven that I had sent you to be a part of his team. He knew he could trust me, so he trusted you. I was working all things out for good. I knew your name and address! You were in the right place at the right time and available to do what was needed. I knew where you were and where you were going to be. Why do you think your train was delayed?

"Count it all joy when assignments change," He said with a grin. "It's all about the testing of your faith. Don't fear. I will be with you!"

"Wow!" said Sam

The Father's Photo

"Don't worry," the Father said.
"I've already taken the photo!"

ON a lovely summer's day, Sam felt the Lord smiling down on her. She looked up at Him and said, "Lord, why are you smiling?"

"Oh, I'm just thinking about your next assignment. After it's finished you'll be smiling too!"

Sam nodded her head in approval!

"OK! So where is it this time?"

"India. I want you to go to India."

"India? Again?"

"I have some serious things to say to some teenagers but I need a voice. Would you go and speak to them, if I put my words in your mouth?"

"Yes Lord. You know I'll go," she said, knowing that He was going to walk with her and care for her in spite of hot curries and unfamiliar customs.

With one suitcase full of children's Bible stories, and the other full of clothes, Sam made her way to the airport. By the time she boarded the plane a guitar had joined the suitcases.

Not long after her arrival in India she was asked to speak to 200 children and teenagers who were part of a large congregation in the city of Visak.

Sharing the love of Jesus with them Sam explained that she had grown up in an orphanage, and didn't know who her father was, and that she had met Jesus one day when a schoolteacher took her to a children's Christian camp.

She sensed God's Holy Spirit settle upon the children as she gently unfolded the truth about God's love.

"He wants to be your friend forever," she told them, "but the choice is yours."

Two hundred children said, "Yes," when invited to give their lives to Jesus. As His peace and love filled them they knew they were now God's children and He was their Heavenly Father, forever!

As the Holy Spirit was drawing the children into a deeper relationship with God, Sam decided to challenge a group of 30 teenagers sitting at the back, asking if they were willing to live for Jesus, even if it meant losing their lives for Him. Thirty teenagers walked to the front of the meeting and knelt down. One by one, with tears streaming down their faces and hands raised they began to pray. Holiness invaded the atmosphere. Sam asked if they were willing to walk the martyr's pathway. All the teenagers began weeping as they placed their lives into God's hands. "Not our will but yours be done," they said.

As Sam looked at the praying children she realised she had the makings of a great photo to present at a missions conference she would be attending in England soon after leaving India. But she was hopelessly penned in by small praying bodies and her camera was inaccessible on the platform behind her.

"Lord!" she exclaimed. "I want to take a photo for the mission conference, but my camera is on the stage back there and I can't climb up to get it."

His answer was immediate. "It's all OK," He said. "I've already taken one!" Sam burst out laughing. The sound of her laughter rose into the air and seemed to ricochet round the roof of the building, "The Lord's taken a photo! The Lord's taken a photo!" Her heart rejoiced.

The meeting was coming to an end; the children were getting up and the atmosphere was returning to normal. As people began to chatter Sam left the auditorium, and made her way to the car park.

Suddenly God spoke again. "Actually, I didn't just take a photo, I took a video!" For just a second Sam was too surprised to speak. Then, holding her sides, she doubled over laughing! "He 's taken a video! He's taken a video!" she shouted.

From that moment on, Sam knew that the Lord recorded every child's prayer, every tear and every expression – never to be forgotten!

Sam might forget where she had been, what she had seen, and what she had heard, but God would never forget!

God doesn't just take photos, He takes videos! He sees all and knows all! Everything is visible to Him. Nothing happens without Him seeing and knowing!

"Father, you were right. You told me I would be smiling at the end of this. But you didn't just make me smile, you made me laugh out loud! I almost split my sides! You saved all those lovely children and you helped them give their lives to you totally, and you took a picture. Wow! Thank you for having such a sense of humour. Not just a photo, but a video! No wonder you sit in the heavens and laugh. You are wonderful!"

The Father's Choice

The Prime Minister whispered to Sam,
"Is this what we call the Holy Spirit?"

"SAM, what would you *like* to do for me?" asked the Father.

"Hmmm! That's an interesting one!" she thought. Then from deep in her heart a response came, "I would like to stand next to someone in high office who is seeking you but can't find you."

The Father, hearing Sam's request, already had a plan. He knew exactly how to answer her prayer!

"Sam," He said, "I am going to arrange some meetings for you. Prepare yourself, but, be aware, all will not be as it seems!"

"Wow! Father! This adventure sounds exciting."

"OK, get yourself ready and I will send you."

It wasn't long before Sam and her friend received an invitation to speak at two national intercession conferences in a nation they had previously visited. With great excitement they boarded the plane, not knowing what God had in store for them!

On arrival they were taken to one of the meetings. It seemed ordinary enough. As people assembled Sam looked around and noticed one of the women looked very familiar. "I'm not sure she's made friends with Jesus," Sam thought. "I wonder why she's here?"

The next minute the lady called out, "Sam, do you remember me?"

Within seconds Sam recognised the lady's voice. She was a senior government official!

"Oh, no," she thought, "if this lady is a government official then who are all these friends she's sitting with?" It didn't take long for Sam to realise that all the people present were members of Parliament, their secretaries and staff. She quickly changed her message and began to build up their faith. "Godliness exalts a nation!" she declared. "When it goes well with the righteous, the city rejoices!"

The next day the Prime Minister and his staff attended. As Sam spoke she was awe-struck. God's love, peace and presence came! For about 10 minutes a hush filled the room and no-one moved. Standing next to Sam, the Prime Minister leaned over and whispered "Is this what we call the Holy Spirit?"

"Yes," Sam whispered back, "This is the Holy Spirit. He is with us."

That afternoon MPs, secretaries and staff received God's love and forgiveness. Those who did not know Him became His friends.

As the atmosphere slowly lifted and the meeting came to a close the Prime Minister called for a group photo. People took their positions, and Sam and her friend stood off to the side. Suddenly the Prime Minister shouted! "Sam, come and stand next to me!" Sam wriggled her way into the middle of the group, and the shutter button clicked. As more photos were being taken, Sam asked the Lord a few questions.

"Father, what am I doing here in the middle of this photo?"

"Sam, you asked me to place you next to people in high office, who are seeking me but can't find me. All I'm doing is answering your prayer!"

"Lord, you are so clever! How did you know I was going to come over here and meet these people? I thought I was coming to teach about prayer."

"I know. I like giving my children surprises! I have a lot of surprises ready for those who love me! Didn't you enjoy my presence? I was letting the leaders know that I loved them. I knew everyone's name and their ways. I knew you were the one to speak for me, that was why I sent you. Thank you for not running away. Whatever is impossible for you, is possible for me!"

Sam, scratching her forehead and shaking her head, realised He had done it again. As usual His goodness and His planning were perfect. He had revealed himself to leaders of government and had, at the same time, with great pleasure, answered her prayer.

The Father's House

"I can't wait to have more friends to spend eternity with," said the Father. "I have even built them houses to live in!"

"You have!!?" said Sam astonished.

"SAM, would you go into all the world and tell others about me?"

God loves every nation and race and ethnic group. He wants them to be with Him in heaven so He can enjoy their company forever. He loves the angels and they do His will, but He loves it more when people willingly love and serve Him.

"Sam, will you go into all the world and preach the good news of my love? I can't wait to have more friends to spend eternity with. I have even built them houses to live in!"

"You *have*?" said Sam.

"Yes! The houses are going to be in a city called the New Jerusalem. I have built this city already. It is in heaven, waiting for me to bring it down to the earth. Each person will have their own house, and the streets in this city are made of pure gold!"

"Wow! Lord, that's incredible! You mean, all those people who have given you their lives and asked you to forgive their sins, and are pleasing you in the way they live, will be given a house to live in, prepared by you?"

"Yes, that's right," He responded with delight. "In that city there will be no more darkness, no tears, no pain, and no death. My presence, light and love will light up the city. I will give good gifts to my children and they will enjoy eternal life with me, and I will be their Father forever."

Sam was speechless.

"To live with you Father, not just here on the earth but also in heaven. That's so exciting! Wow!

"So, Lord," Sam continued, "whether I live or whether I die, am I always yours?"

"Yes, whether you live or die you are mine forever. When you asked me to live in you, I gave you my free gift of eternal life for now and always. My relationship with you in heaven will just be a continuation of my life with you on earth – just better! The joy you know now will continue on into heaven. My presence, my love, my peace, these will all continue with you to your new eternal home. I have placed eternity in your heart. Where I am, you will also be."

Sam, so excited about eternal life, immediately placed her life and future straight back into God's hands.

"Father?"

"Yes, Sam."

"Can I share with you a song I've writtten?"

"Of course you can."

Please give me a vision of Jesus
That nothing on earth can dim.
Fill my whole soul and spirit,
With the knowledge that I have Him.

That even though mind and body
Are weak on this mortal way
Please give to my heart such a longing
That nothing can take away.

Help me be conscious of Jesus
And know He's there above,
Pleading for me in glory,
Revealing to me His love.

A faith that never weakens,
And a love that never grows dim,
A consciousness always growing
Of a deepening love for Him.

Please show me much more of my Saviour.
Please give me more faith to see
– untouched by a world of darkness – a constant reality'.

The Father's heart was moved by Sam's song. He knew she loved Him. No matter what difficulties laid ahead, He knew she wanted to live for Him. He laid down His life for her and she was willing to lay down her life for Him.

Sam would often quote a Bible verse:

I have been crucified with Christ. I myself no longer live, but Christ lives in me. So I live my life in this earthly body by trusting in the Son of God, who loved me and gave himself for me. (Galatians 2 v 19b – 20)

Sam thought for a moment. "My life is not my own. You have bought me with the precious blood of your Son, Jesus. Thank you Father for loving me."

She decided to add a few more lines to her song.

Father, wherever you lead me, I will go,
Over the mountains, or through the snow,
Into the valleys down below,
Where you lead me I will go.

The Author's Comments

I hope you have enjoyed journeying with me through these pages. May the joy I have living with God be yours as well. Be all that God has intended you to be! Nothing short of His best!

If you would like to get to know Him as your personal friend, you can. All you have to do is speak to Him! Let me help you do that. Here's how:

"Father in heaven. Thank you for sending your Son Jesus down to this earth to die for my sin. Thank you for loving me. I know you know my name and everything about me, so I come to you today. Please forgive me. Come into my heart and fill me with your joy! Take my sins away so I can be your friend! I thank you for your gift of eternal life so I

can be with you forever. I want to know you and love you!
Thank you Jesus for loving me. I give you my life!"

Now, sit quietly in His presence. Let Him forgive you and fill you with His peace. Your Heavenly Father has heard your prayer. You now have a personal, supernatural relationship with the living God!

Go and tell someone that you are His child and He is your Father! As you tell others about Jesus He talks to His Father in heaven about you. Go! Tell your friends about Him!

The Greatest Adventure of your life has just begun!

If you want to contact Bunty email her at
tgreatestadventure@yahoo.com

The Father's Desire

Rejoice always.
Pray without ceasing.
In everything give thanks.

For this is the will of God in Christ Jesus for you.
(I Thessalonians 5:16-18)

If you do these three things, His will and plans for your life
will become clear.

May He take you on great adventures!

God bless you.

Bible verses to learn

Jesus said: If you follow me
I will make you fishers of men

And this is the way to have eternal life – to know you, the
only true God, and Jesus Christ, the one you sent to earth.
John 17 :3

Show me the right path, O Lord; point out the road for me to
follow. Lead me by your truth and teach me, for you are the
God who saves me. All day long I put my hope in you.
Psalm 25:4 – 5

... be strong and immovable. Always work enthusiastically
for the Lord, for you know that nothing you do for the Lord is
ever useless.
I Corinthians 15:58

For God loved the world so much that he gave his one and
only Son, so that everyone who believes in him will not perish
but have eternal life.
John 3:16

(NLT)